BeR

Please renew or return items by the date
shown on your receipt

www.hertfordshire.gov.uk/libraries

Renewals and enquiries: 0300 123 4049

Textphone for hearing or 0300 123 4041
speech impaired users:

L32 11.16

Let's Talk About
The Birds And
The Bees

Dedicated to Neil – my very grown up friend

Featherstone Education
An imprint of Bloomsbury Publishing Plc

50 Bedford Square
London
WC1B 3DP
UK

1385 Broadway
New York
NY 10018
USA

www.bloomsbury.com

FEATHERSTONE and the Featherstone logo are trademarks of Bloomsbury Publishing Plc

First published in Great Britain 2017

Copyright © Molly Potter, 2017
Illustrations copyright © Sarah Jennings, 2017

Molly Potter has asserted her right under the Copyright, Designs and Patents Act, 1988, to be identified as Author of this work.

A catalogue record for this book is available from the British Library.

ISBN
HB: 978-1-4729-4641-6
ePDF: 978-1-4729-4644-7

2 4 6 8 10 9 7 5 3 1

Printed and bound in China by Leo Paper Products, Heshan, Guangdong

This book is produced using paper that is made from wood grown in managed, sustainable forests. It is natural, renewable and recyclable. The logging and manufacturing processes conform to the environmental regulations of the country of origin.

To find out more about our authors and books visit www.bloomsbury.com. Here you will find extracts, author interviews, details of forthcoming events and the option to sign up for our newsletters.

Let's Talk About The Birds And The Bees

Molly Potter

Illustrated by Sarah Jennings

FEATHERSTONE
AN IMPRINT OF BLOOMSBURY
LONDON OXFORD NEW YORK NEW DELHI SYDNEY

What you'll find in this book

Stuff for grown ups to read

What's covered in this book...

Where do babies come from and how are they made?

Lots of children ask questions like this and it's very normal to be really interested in the answers. This book will explain everything you need to know with lots of pictures and diagrams to help illustrate the answers.

What happens to my body as I grow up?

You might also have wondered why men's and women's bodies are different or why adult's bodies are a different size and shape to children's bodies. Have you ever wondered how a baby grows inside its mummy or how it's actually born? This book will explain these things and much, much more.

Do you wonder what makes a family or what it's like to be a parent?

Do you sometimes wonder what will change as you grow up or what it's like to be a parent? It's good to think about these things and this book will help you understand them even more.

Don't get confused

Because this book answers lots of questions, you might like to sit down with an adult and share two or three pages at a time. You can then go away and think about what you've read. If you are confused by anything, you can go back and ask the adult more questions until you are happy with what you understand.

IT'S GOOD TO KNOW...

For some people sex is a very private thing and talking about it embarrasses them. You might sometimes find adults who are not happy to talk about the topics covered in this book. This book is called, 'Let's Talk About The Birds And The Bees' because some people say 'birds and bees' instead of saying sex!

How are girls and boys different?

When young girls and boys are dressed, they look quite similar. Most body parts are the same.

Girls are more likely to have long hair but both girls and boys can have long or short hair.

The main difference between girls and boys is found between their legs and you can't see it when they're dressed!

What are these differences?

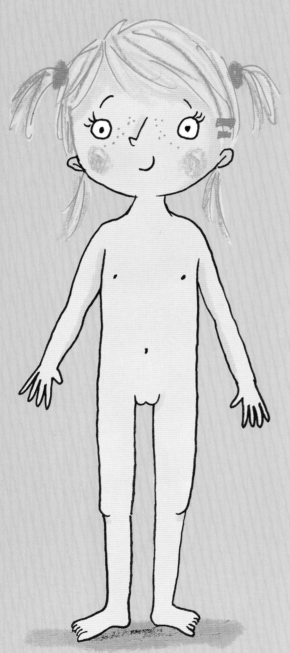

A girl has a vagina that is like a tube that goes inside her body with an open end between her legs.

Boys have a penis that sticks out. He uses his penis to pee. Behind his penis are testicles.

Families often use different names for this part of a girl's body but vagina is the proper name.

Families often have other names for a penis – like 'willy' – but penis is the proper name.

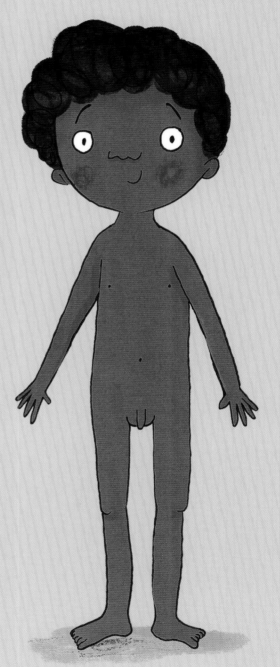

How are grown ups different from children?

Grown ups are usually bigger than children.
Children are still growing but grown ups have stopped.

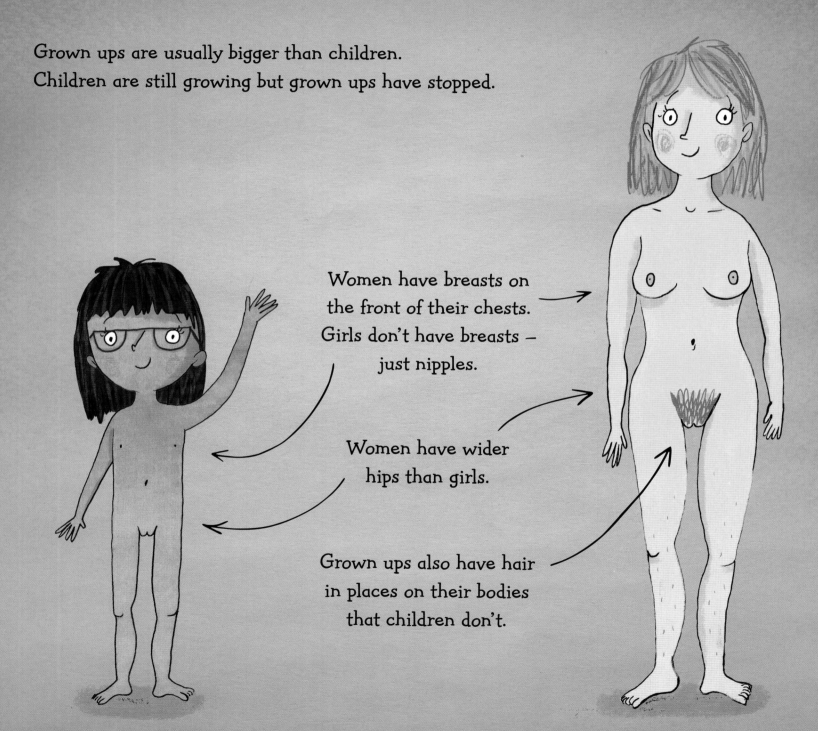

Women have breasts on the front of their chests. Girls don't have breasts – just nipples.

Women have wider hips than girls.

Grown ups also have hair in places on their bodies that children don't.

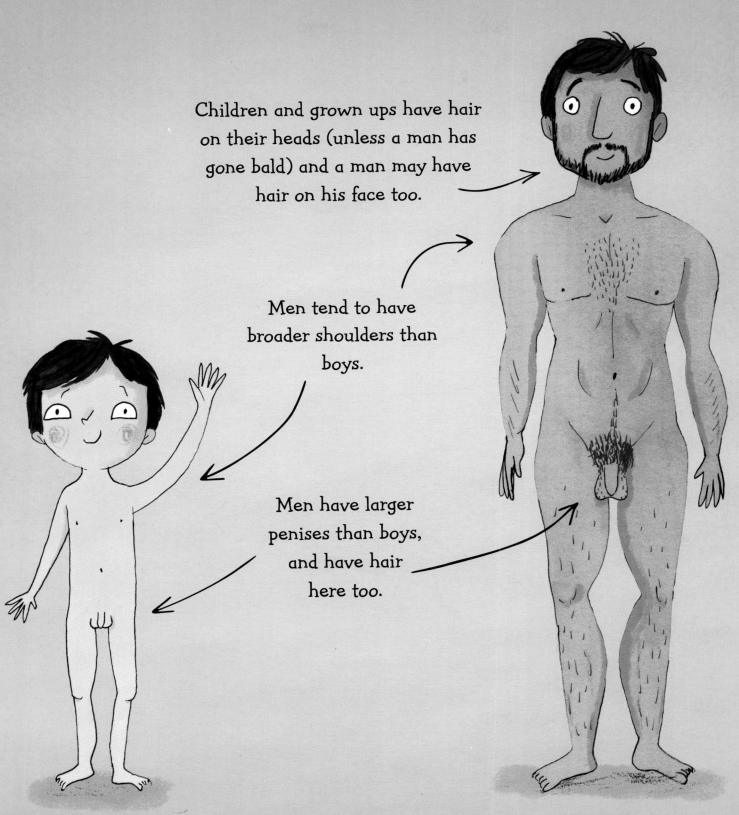

Children and grown ups have hair on their heads (unless a man has gone bald) and a man may have hair on his face too.

Men tend to have broader shoulders than boys.

Men have larger penises than boys, and have hair here too.

Which parts of our bodies are private?

Adults tend not to show certain parts of their bodies in public. For men, it's the area covered by their swimming trunks.

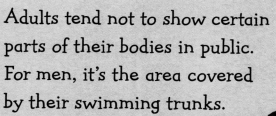

For women, these are the parts covered by a bikini or swimsuit.

Some people choose to keep more parts of their bodies covered in public because of what they believe.

DON'T FORGET
You don't have to show any part of your body to another person if you don't want to. Your body belongs to you.

When is touching OK?

Hugs and kisses can feel really nice from people we know well. However, not all touching feels nice or right. If anyone touches you and it doesn't feel right, you need to make it stop.

If you can't make it stop, you need to keep telling adults you trust until one of them makes it stop.

If anyone touches you in any of your private areas and tells you to keep it a secret, you should tell someone you trust even if you feel scared.

DON'T FORGET
If anyone touches you in a way that you don't like, you need to keep telling someone that you trust until it stops.

Why are children's and adult's bodies different?

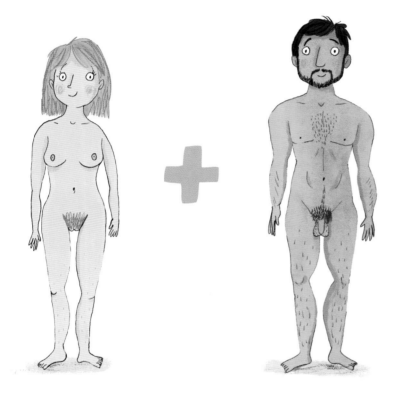

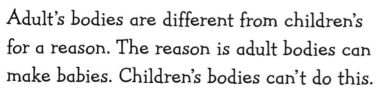

Adult's bodies are different from children's for a reason. The reason is adult bodies can make babies. Children's bodies can't do this.

Adults are also bigger and stronger than children which helps to make them good at looking after their children.

When do children's bodies turn into adult's bodies?

Children start as babies and they keep growing until they become an adult.

At about the age of 11 for girls and 13 for boys, children's bodies not only grow but they also start to change. These changes are called puberty.

Some of the changes at puberty happen to both girls and boys, some just to girls and others just to boys. You can read about these changes on the following pages.

DID YOU KNOW?
Puberty usually takes about two years - so the changes don't happen really suddenly.

How does a **girl change** when she reaches puberty?

She will have a growth spurt.

Her face will start to look more adult.

She will sweat more and her hair might become greasy.

She might get spots on her face.

↑

Me when I was 7 years old

16

Hair starts to grow under her arms and in the area between her legs. Some women shave this hair off.

Her hips become wider and she becomes more curvy as she puts on weight.

She grows breasts.

Her periods start. This is where a small amount of blood comes out of her vagina over a few days each month. This can seem a bit strange at first but she soon gets used to it.

DID YOU KNOW?
When a girl has been through puberty, she usually stops growing any taller.

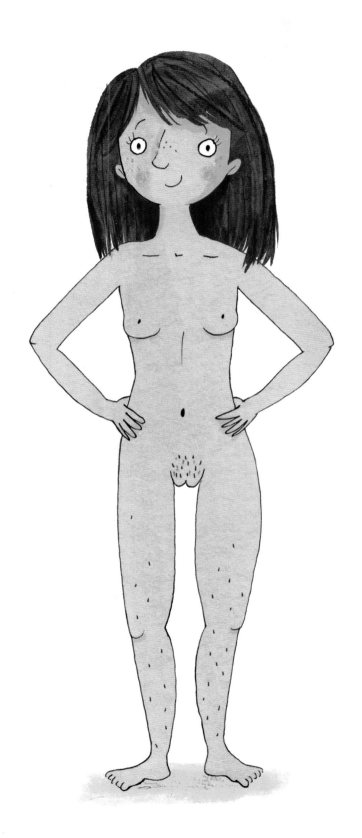

How does a **boy change** when he reaches puberty?

He will sweat more and his hair might become greasy.

Hair will start to grow on his face so that he might choose to shave.

He might get spots on his face.

His voice becomes deeper.

Me when I was 7 years old

18

His shoulders will grow broader and his muscles bigger.

Hair also starts to grow under his arms, in the area between his legs and sometimes on his chest as well.

He starts to make semen – a liquid that comes out of the end of his penis.

He will have a growth spurt and start to look more adult. A growth spurt is when a child grows a lot in a short time.

DID YOU KNOW?

Some teenage boys might grow as much as an inch every month for about a year during puberty. That's a lot of growing!

What does puberty feel like?

Puberty can be a difficult time for some teenagers.

It can be a time when young people feel a bit shy about all the changes happening to their bodies.

It can also make some teenagers a bit moody – really happy one minute and grumpy the next.

Some children go through puberty at a younger age than their friends and this can make them feel a bit different.

Some children go through puberty later than their friends and this can make them feel a bit different too.

Once they reach puberty teenagers realise they have to wash more or they will start to smell.

It's a funny in-between time because a person is no longer a child but not yet an adult.

Nobody should tease anyone about the changes that happen at puberty.

How do grown ups make a baby?

As we have seen, men have a penis and women have a vagina.

Most of the time a man's penis is floppy and dangles between his legs. Sometimes though when mummies and daddies cuddle in bed, the daddy's penis gets firm and sticks up instead of down. This means that the daddy's penis can be pushed inside the mummy's vagina. This usually feels nice for both of them and it's what we call sex.

22

During sex a small amount of liquid called semen comes out of the end of the man's penis.

This liquid has tiny sperm in it that are the man's seeds needed to make a baby. Sperm look like tadpoles but are much smaller.

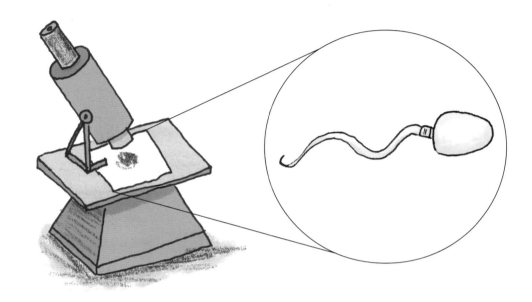

The sperm swim up inside the woman and can sometimes make a baby.

The rest of the baby making happens inside the mummy after the sperm has gone inside her.

What makes a baby?

You need sperm and an egg to make a baby. Both are tiny.

Sperm come out here

Eggs come from here

The sperm come from the man. Sperm are in the semen that comes out of the end of a man's penis when he has sex.

The egg comes from the woman. The eggs are stored inside her. They are made in a place called an ovary. She has two of these.

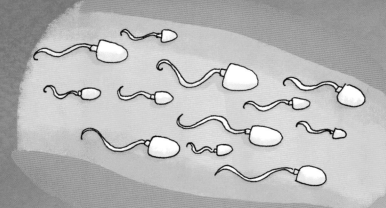

Once the sperm get inside the woman during sex, they travel inside her towards the egg.

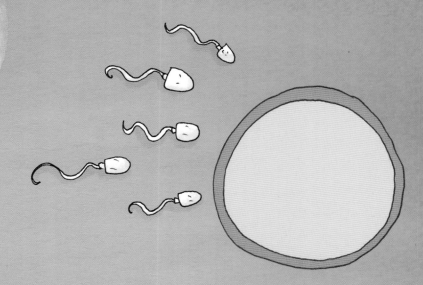

Sperm have tails like tiny tadpoles and they swim towards the egg.

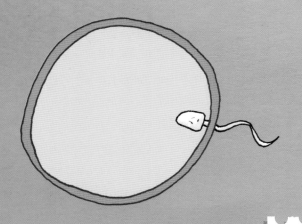

When a sperm and an egg get together a baby starts to form.

Sometimes men and women are trying to make a baby when they have sex but sometimes it just happens and it's a surprise.

DID YOU KNOW?
Sometimes the egg and sperm are put together outside the body and then put into the woman's body to grow.

Is a baby made every time a man and woman have sex?

Sex is not just about making babies. When two people love each other, sex can make them feel even closer. Sex is sometimes called 'making love'.

Sex can be fun and enjoyable and men and women like having sex just for how nice it feels. They don't always want to make a baby when they have sex.

An egg is only ready to turn into a baby about once a month so a woman doesn't make a baby every time sperm swim inside her. Doctors and nurses can also give men and women special things that stop a baby happening.

This means two people can have sex and not make a baby.

Having sex is a private thing and it most often happens in a grown up's bedroom with the door shut!

How do babies grow before they are born?

Babies develop in a special baby-growing place called a womb. The womb is inside a mummy.

The baby is tiny at first and the mummy doesn't look pregnant but then, over nine months the baby grows and the mummy's tummy starts to get bigger and bigger.

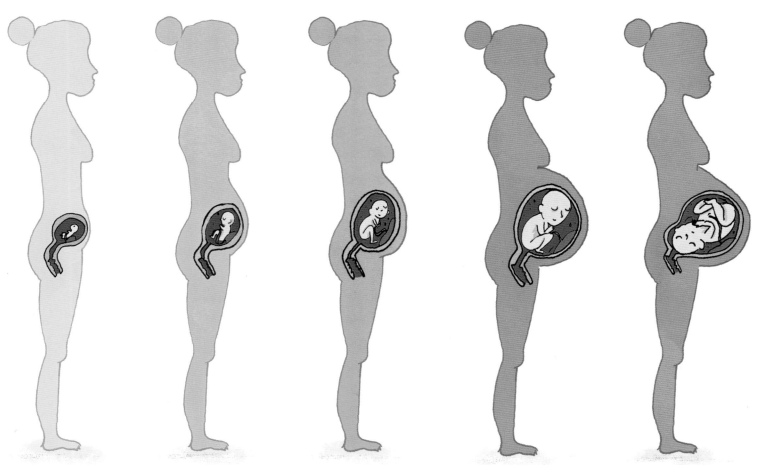

This is the womb

The womb stretches as the baby grows. A mummy's body goes through lots of changes as a baby grows inside her. She can feel very large and uncomfortable towards the end of her pregnancy.

When the baby is inside the womb the baby gets all it needs through a tube called the umbilical cord.

Umbilical cord

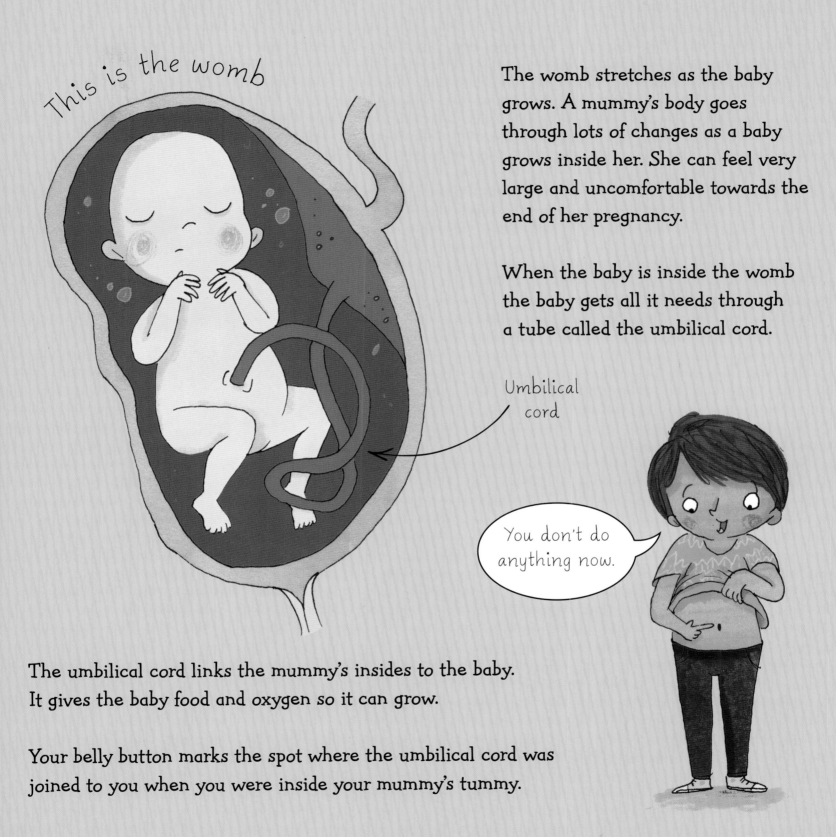

You don't do anything now.

The umbilical cord links the mummy's insides to the baby. It gives the baby food and oxygen so it can grow.

Your belly button marks the spot where the umbilical cord was joined to you when you were inside your mummy's tummy.

How are babies born?

After about nine months, the baby has grown enough and is ready to be born.

The mummy will know that the baby is on its way because she will go into labour. Labour is what the mummy's body has to do to get the baby out of her womb and into the world.

30

Labour can take anything from about an hour to a day or more. Labour is usually painful for the mummy but doctors can do things to help with the pain.

After some time in labour the mummy's body is ready to have the baby. Her vagina has become wide enough for the baby's head to come out and the mummy pushes really hard until the baby is born.

Some babies are born by caesarean section. This is where doctors cut a small hole in the mummy's tummy to get the baby out.

What are babies like?

When babies are first born, they usually sleep a lot.

Babies can do very little for themselves and they need lots of care from a grown up.

For food, a baby only drinks milk at first – either from its mummy's breast or a bottle.

All babies cry – it's their only way of saying they need something.

Babies start to smile at about six weeks old.

A baby starts to eat solid food at about six months.

A baby learns to walk when he or she is about a year old.

Slowly a baby learns to speak – starting with one or two words and then adding more words as she or he gets older.

Mama!

REMEMBER

If you get a baby brother or sister, it can take some getting used to.
It also means you have to share the grown ups in your life with the new baby.

What happens when you grow up?

As you grow up, you don't just get bigger. You also get better and better at looking after yourself.

At different ages you will like different things.

You also learn to do more things for yourself.

When you become a teenager, you will start fancying other people.

34

Eventually you won't need your parents to look after you at all. You will probably leave home once you are a grown up.

You might one day have children of your own.

35

What's love all about?

Love is what you feel when you really, really adore someone.

When you love someone, thinking about them can make you smile and feel warm and fluttery inside.

You are very special to the people who love you.

There are lots of different kinds of love.

Love for your family is about them being there for you and caring about you.

Grown ups and teenagers can fall in love romantically with people who are not in their family.

When teenagers and grown ups fall in love, they find each other attractive.

You're gorgeous.

When grown ups love each other romantically, they sometimes kiss, touch, cuddle and have sex with each other.

DID YOU KNOW?
When a man loves a man or a woman loves a woman, we call this a gay relationship.

What's a family and how can they be different?

A family is a group of people who are related to each other and who tend to all live in the same house.

People in a family usually love and look after each other and spend time together.

Some families have lots of children – others just one.

Sometimes children spend time in two different family homes if their parents are no longer together.

Some children live with step or half brothers and sisters.

Some families have two mums or two dads.

Some families have just one parent or carer, others have two.

Some children are adopted.

REMEMBER
You get very used to the way your family does things. When you visit your friends' families, you might find that they do some things the same and some things differently.

What's it like being a parent?

Being a parent is not an easy job. Once a baby comes along, a parent has to look after him or her all the time. Parents have to make sure their babies and children are safe, warm, healthy, clean, fed, entertained and feel loved. That's lots of jobs!

40

Parents help their children to learn to behave well.

Parents can spend a lot of time with their children playing and having fun.

Parents look after their children until they are ready to look after themselves.

Being a parent can also be a wonderful job!

Why do some parents' relationships sometimes go wrong?

When two people first fall in love they really enjoy being together.

Sometimes though, after a while, some people fall out of love.

When this happens, the good feelings between them disappear and they struggle to be together.

This can be because they stop being as nice to each other as they were when they first got together or because they want different things.

I want to move abroad

Sometimes parents argue all the time and don't make up and sometimes one or both of them fall in love with someone else.

When two people make each other unhappy more than they make each other happy, they often split up. When parents split up, there's always lots of feelings to deal with. It can seem really difficult at first but after a while everyone usually gets used to the changes and feels better.

Why talking to your child about sex, gender and relationships is a good thing

Children learn about sex and relationships from a variety of sources (older siblings, the media, friends, etc). Much of the information they receive is inaccurate or gives them unhealthy messages. It's better to give them accurate information than to leave them confused or misinformed.

Sex can potentially be harmful, with the risk of STIs for example, but so can crossing the road! Imagine if talking about crossing the road safely caused embarrassment, would that stop you from teaching your child road safety?

Research has shown that children who have discussed sex and relationships from an early age are more prepared for puberty and body changes, more likely to delay having early sex and more likely to use condoms and contraception.

Most children want their parents or carers to be the main source of information about sex and relationships.

If you are relaxed and open when it comes to talking about bodies, gender, sex and relationships with your child, he or she is more likely to turn to you when they need advice or questions answered about these issues.

Common anxieties parents and carers share

Won't talking about sex encourage my child to experiment?

Research shows this is certainly not the case. Children and young people who have never learnt about sex are more likely to 'fall prey' to negative sexual experiences.

Won't this taint my child's innocence?

Parents/carers that have discussed sex and how babies are made with their children at a very young age would argue that their children are no less innocent for having this information. This information is not harmful. Talking openly about sex early in a child's life teaches them that you are prepared to talk about it. It shows that parents are people they can turn to for help and support should they need it, at any point in their lives.

Won't this information worry my child?

Not if it's discussed sensitively with lots of opportunities for questions. The way many people were taught in the past often left children worried and confused.

I just get too embarrassed.

Start conversations while doing something else (e.g. washing up or in the car) so you can avoid eye contact. Once underway, you should find the conversation gets more relaxed and then you'll find sharing this book much easier.

It just feels wrong talking to kids about sex.

Nearly everyone has a strong reaction to talking about sex with children. Some people aren't comfortable talking about sex in an open and sensitive way. This discomfort can prevent much needed conversations and can contribute to leaving our young people in the dark about what a positive sexual experience should be and therefore vulnerable to negative experiences.

I don't know what to say.

This book will help guide you with what to say about each carefully selected topic. You can start with the questions on page 6-7 and ask your child what they would like to find out about first.

What our children are learning anyway (often without adults knowing).

Children and young people are bombarded with information about sex, relationships and gender from a variety of sources (e.g. TV adverts, graffiti, shop displays/posters, the internet, computer games, pop video images, their school friends, older brothers and sisters etc.). Some of the messages children receive from these sources are not accurate or realistic and, in the absence of adults to help them process this information, they can often be left confused or with 'unhealthy' ideas.

The media, for example, can lead children and young people to believe:

- Everyone is having sex all the time.

- Sex is only ever exciting, fun, easy and uncomplicated.

- You don't need to be responsible about sex.

- Sex is something that is everywhere but you shouldn't talk about it openly or sensitively.

- To be a successful man, you have to have sex with lots of women.

- To be a successful woman, you must look sexy.

- Most teenagers start having sex at a young age.

- Sex is something we shouldn't be serious about.

If your child feels he or she can talk to you openly about these topics, they are more likely to receive healthier messages and accurate information.

What children say they want

They want parents and carers who...

- Initiate conversations about these topics.
- Tell the truth (even when it's embarrassing or awkward).
- Start talking about these topics to young children so it becomes comfortable and children feel they can ask questions about anything.
- Appear comfortable when talking about sex and body parts so children feel they can ask questions – including what different words mean.
- Talk privately about these topics because that makes it easier.
- Don't tease or laugh about anything misunderstood or share the content of the conversation with other people.
- Admit when they don't know something instead of making things up or going quiet.
- Let them freely express opinions about these issues and not be upset if they disagree.
- Provide them with books and leaflets to look at.
- Don't give them too much information at once as that can be overwhelming.

Other helpful tips for talking to your child

You, like everyone, will have your own views about sex and relationships. You can discuss these views with your child and you can listen to your child's views. However, try to develop a tolerance for views that are different from yours. Your child may well 'test' you at some point so it's best not to be too judgemental towards different viewpoints as this may prevent open communication between you and your child later on.

As well as acknowledging family names, try using the correct terms for body parts e.g. vagina, clitoris, penis and testicles as this will be what your child's school uses in Sex and Relationships Education (SRE) lessons.

As your child gets older use TV soaps, teenage magazines, the news etc. to raise topics relating to sex, body image and relationships.

Very young children show curiosity about their own and other people's bodies e.g. playing doctors and nurses – be careful how you react to any curiosity as you might give children the message that certain parts of the body are 'bad'.

Tell your children that you are always happy to answer any questions they have about sex, bodies and relationships.

If you are comfortable with this, share personal experiences and feelings of your own. For example, crushes, body image, the changes of puberty, first girlfriends/boyfriends etc.

Never dismiss any anxieties your child has as they will be very real for them – even if they seem silly to you.